A Place of Sense

Rick Vivian

Matador

A Place of Sense

Little-known Meanings of British Place Names

Rick Vivian

Copyright © 2018 Rick Vivian
The moral right of the author has been asserted.

Apart from any fair dealing for the purposes of research or private study, or criticism or review, as permitted under the Copyright, Designs and Patents Act 1988, this publication may only be reproduced, stored or transmitted, in any form or by any means, with the prior permission in writing of the publishers, or in the case of reprographic reproduction in accordance with the terms of licences issued by the Copyright Licensing Agency. Enquiries concerning reproduction outside those terms should be sent to the publishers.

This is a work of fiction. Names, characters, businesses, places, events and incidents are either the products of the author's imagination or used in a fictitious manner. Any resemblance to actual persons, living or dead, or actual events is purely coincidental.

Matador
9 Priory Business Park,
Wistow Road, Kibworth Beauchamp,
Leicestershire. LE8 0RX
Tel: 0116 279 2299
Email: books@troubador.co.uk
Web: www.troubador.co.uk/matador
Twitter: @matadorbooks

ISBN 9781788037563

British Library Cataloguing in Publication Data.
A catalogue record for this book is available from the British Library.

Printed and Bound in the UK by 4Edge Limited
Typeset in Baskerville Regular 12pt by Troubador Publishing Ltd, Leicester, UK

Matador is an imprint of Troubador Publishing Ltd

*For my four wonderful children
Michael, Andrew, Rachael and Gregory*

Author's note

None of the place names in this document are imaginary and all may be found on an Ordnance Survey map.

Nonetheless, this is a work of fiction and the associated definitions and attributions have absolutely no connection whatsoever with the places they share a name with – and, in many cases, little connection with the truth either.

Where descriptions are set in a specific place it is not because I believe that the location is more likely to exhibit the attributes described, it is simply an appreciative salute to that part of the country which is 'home' to the place named.

Similarly, all characters are imaginary and bear no relation to real persons living or dead – which is a bit of a shame in some cases.

Introduction

Homographs are all around us. Native English speakers negotiate them oblivious to their intricacies, where an English-language student, if faced with 'bow', has to decide, consciously, whether to tie an ornate knot or bend double.

There are over 150 homographs in common use. Consider: 'bow' meaning bow or bow, 'object' meaning object or object, 'moped' meaning moped or moped; the list goes on (in some documents, more helpfully).

What is commonly overlooked is that this is true for words that are names, every bit as much as for those that are not.

As has been alluded to above there are many documents detailing and comparing the meanings of non-titular homographs; far fewer do so for names. This work seeks to redress that balance, at least to a small degree. I hope it has the desired effect (not to be confused with effect).

A

ABERFAN *n.*:
Swedish groupie

ABINGER HAMMER *n.*:
An earth-shaking hangover

ACHA *n.*:
Western Scottish dialect for a sneeze

ACHA MOR *n.*:
Western Scottish dialect for a bad cold

ACKLE *n.*:
A jaunty feather for one's 'at

ACTON *n.*:
(arch.) Large wooden board placed on low trestles and used as a stage by troupes of strolling players

ACTON TRUSSEL *n.*:
(arch.) an Acton (qv.) fitted with hidden trapdoors and used by escapologists and magicians

ADBOLTON *v.*:
Carry out DIY home security improvements

ADDERLY *adv.* :
In the manner of a snake

AIRIELAND *n.* :
Magical place of tale and fable inhabited by Airies (furry little creatures with wings)

ALDWINCLE *n.* :
Northamptonshire argot; affectionate name for a village's 'old character'. Traditionally the Aldwincle had first call on 'his' corner seat in the pub and rarely had to buy a drink (never, for others). Latterly, in more bureaucratically inclined communities this epithet is reserved for the Senior Village Idiot

ALFOLD CROSSWAYS *n.* :
A short-lived labour movement founded in Surrey in the late 19th century. At that time the delights of the near Continent, particularly Paris, were becoming 'the rage' with the nation's 'bright young things' who returned from their frolics abroad looking for the same style at home. For the previous several centuries, British maids and chamber-maids (who supported the established country house parties and hotel naughty weekends) had been taught to fold bedding in the traditional, Crossways, British style, preferred because when rolling over, one was less inclined to get tangled in the bedding, carrying it with one. The French Lengthways style, which promoted entanglement, and usually brought one's bed-mate with the

bedding, was what the 'new travellers' wanted. Thus, fearing for their livelihood, the Surrey domestics formed the Alfold Crossways movement and refused to make beds 'in the French style'. The dispute was quickly settled thanks to the enterprising landlord of the Dog & Missionary in Dippenhall. He agreed with his worker that she should continue to fold bedding and make beds crossways but, at the request of an incoming guest, she would go to the room and rotate the bedding by 90 degrees. Recognising that this provided more work and job security for the maids, it was quickly generally adopted and the movement disbanded. Interestingly, the arrangement proved remarkably popular with single male guests

AMOTHERBY *n.* :
A baby bee's best friend

ARDECHIVE *n.* :
Common accompaniment to 'ard cheese

ARDENTINNY *n.* :
Tin

ASPULL *n.* :
Like a leg-pull, but ruder

AYNHO *adv. & conj.* :
Norfolk dialect meaning notwithstanding or without method

B

BACK OF KEPPOCH *n.*:
(arch.) Crude agricultural rainwear made of sacking

BACKIES *n. pl.*:
Selfies taken from behind (presumably to show the view in front of the photographer)

BADLIPSTER *n.*:
Young person (of either sex) not yet skilled in the art of makeup

BALDOCK *n.*:
The small chute that catches the balls in sequence as they are ejected from the National Lottery machine

BANNOCKBURN *n.*:
Injury caused by removing scones from a bread-oven without suitable protective clothing

BARDRAINNEY *n.*:
The sink behind a pub counter

BARTON IN THE BEANS *n.*:
Manufacturing problem in the Heinz factory

BAWDSEY *adj. & adv.* :
Like or in the manner of: a brothel, brothel keeper, prostitute

BEESWING *n.* :
Big-band version of 'The Flight of the Bumble Bee'

BENTLEY *adj.* :
Not straight. It is interesting to note that Bentley Colliery was actually named after its unique main lift shaft. Built for an exceptionally fast mechanism, the shaft was dug with a slight curve to allow for lateral acceleration due to the rotation of the Earth

BIG SAND *n.* :
Used to work for me once – nice girl

BOLTON *n.* :
Any aftermarket accessory

BOULGE *n.* :
Permanent lop-sided set of a jacket in which the owner habitually carries a large or heavy object

BLAIRINGONE *n.* :
Raucous motor horn

BLOXWICH *n.* :
Main circuit breaker which allows firefighters to isolate an entire high-rise structure from the electricity supply in an emergency

BOLTON PERCY *n.* :
??
(redacted, Ed.)

BRAN END *n.* :
Soreness of the rectum brought about by too much fibre in the diet

BRIGHTON & HOVE *interj.* :
(arch. 18th cent.) Attack order from the Age of Sail. When a Revenue cutter which had been shadowing a smuggler's craft under cover of darkness succeeded in getting up-wind of its prey, the order, "Brighton & Hove" was given. At that point all the navigation and battle lanterns were lit, the cutter ran down on its prey, ranged alongside and seized it (sometimes).

BROADBOTTOM *n.* :
A sailing craft for cargo with a shallow draft and wide beam, not unlike a Thames barge. Such vessels were considered 'capable of receiving a good load, stable even in rough conditions and easy to handle when the wind gets up.' Latterly this became a slang term for a certain type of barmaid in Thames dockside pubs. How the characteristics of a boat lend themselves to a barmaid is open to speculation.

BROADWAY *n.* :
Though an ancient place name for British settlements, Broadway was rarely found as a street

name before the First World War. That usage was initially introduced by visiting service men (esp. USA) to those roads in communities where innocent, though hospitable and fun-loving, young women would congregate in the evening. A second spate of streets named Broadway occurred during the early 1940s

BUCKERELL *n.* :
Term used (quietly) by a verger when passing the collection plate to the priest after a particularly fruitless collection

BULDOO *n.* :
Just about acceptable term for obvious misinformation imparted innocently by a genteel and gullible relative (such information is most usually gleaned from their favourite newspaper)

BURNHAM-ON-CROUCH *n.* :
Thankfully short-lived condition caused by stinging nettles when attempting to go to the toilet *al fresco* after dark

BURNSIDE *n.* :
The opposite side to that on which you went to sleep while sunbathing

BURSTALL *n.* :
One of the two inevitable outcomes of drinking deeply of champagne while wearing a tightly laced corset

BURTON JOYCE *n.* :
English translation of the title of a French 'art-house' film

BURY *interj.* :
The traditional cry of a player of Bury St Edmunds (qv.) who has succeeded in the quest and won that round. It signals their success and requires that the remaining players should not look or listen whilst he or she arranges another disappearance

BURY St EDMUNDS *n.* :
A particularly violent variant of the game 'Hunt-the-Thimble'.

BUSHEY *n.* :
One of many hairstyles offered, nationally, by beauty salons

BUTTERMERE *n.* :
A trifling gift

C

CALIFORNIA *n.* :
Over-ambitious place-naming initiative by the Norfolk Tourist Board

CALVINE *adj.* :
Like a calf

CAMAS LUINIE *n.* :
(obs.) Fancy dress party briefly fashionable in the late 18th and early 19th century where guests were invited to come attired as inmates of Bedlam

CANLEY *adj.* :
In a tin (e.g. peas canley)

CARDIFF *n.* :
Knitted fashion garment similar to a waistcoat but cropped short just under the bust-line

CARLISLE *n.* :
Open weave material made from tightly wound but absorbent cotton thread, used for making the backs of driving gloves

CARLTON SCROOP *n.* :
(19th cent.) Breathing difficulties experienced

by regular guests in those hotels that were early adopters of air-conditioning, caused by drying of the airways

CAUSEWAY END *n.* :
The point by which you should have stopped.

CHARTWELL *adj.* :
Adept at using PowerPoint

CHENIES *n.* :
Selfies taken by inmates of American penitentiaries

CHERTSEY *n.* :
Quick, shallow genuflection made by a woman towards a person of high social standing or real worldly power. The obvious meagreness of the salute might most commonly be occasioned by a barely concealed lack of respect for the chertseyee or else an urgent desire to get out of his or her sight (and reach) as quickly as possible

CHESHIRE *n.* :
English county which, even before the Domesday Book, was named, with almost unbelievable prescience, after Ernesto 'Che' Guevara, Argentinian Marxist revolutionary. That this fact only came to light late in the drug-fuelled, revolutionary Swinging Sixties may be significant

CHEW MAGNA *v.* :
To masticate, embarrassingly, an ill-advised

mouthful which proves to be far too large to cope with politely and without considerable discomfort

CHIPPING WARDEN *n.* :
The stock-controller in a County Council Highways Department

CLAPHAM COMMON *n.* :
An area originally named Clapham Greensward. Subsequently, more than three centuries of dismissive comments by people living north of the Thames led to its gradual name-shift to Clapham Common

CLENT *adj.* :
A West Midland dialect expression meaning that something 'has been cleaned'

CLEWER *n.* :
Congenitally careless criminal

CLIFF END *n.* :
Regrettably common method of suicide between Eastbourne and Seaford

CLIMPING *n. v.* :
Traditional Chinese method of hair curling

COLD ASHBY *n.* :
The very unpleasant mental symptoms – confusion often accompanied by a burning sensation – experienced when making the sudden and

involuntary switch from a wood-fired AGA to a gas cooker (e.g. going cold ashby)

COOLHAM *n.* :
West Sussex village where all the really wealthy, trendy, 'in' people would like to buy property (though not necessarily live)

COPISTER *n.* :
Person with whom, when at a party and in bladderly extremis, one shares a toilet bowl

CORRIECRAVIE *n.* :
An excessively avid watcher of *Coronation Street*

CORSE LAWN *n.* :
Area of grass resembling my own back garden

CORTON DENHAM *adj.* :
Hooked up on the button of someone else's jeans

COSELEY *adv.* :
Snugly

COSTON *n.* :
Price supplement

COTMANHAY *interj.* :
Over-familiar and ill-advised greeting to the manager of a branch of shops such as *Mothercare*, *Mama's & Papa's*, etc. when hoping to negotiate a discount

COTTERED *adj.* :
Having consumed far too much alcohol for any good to come of it

COUNTESS WEAR *n.* :
National chain of shops specialising in budget outfits for girls attending their School Prom

COURTSEND *n.* :
Little known and rarely used judicial power, never removed from the statute-books, directly equivalent to Transportation, but with no prescribed destination. Analysing where different judges have banished criminals would be an interesting area for academic study

COVENTRY *n.* :
The crime committed by an illegal gathering of witches (e.g. "My lord, these wretched women have been taken in the very act of coventry.")

CREDITON *v.* :
To increase a borrowing or purchasing limit

CRICK *n.* :
(1) Noise made by a creaking door when moved very slightly by a draft; (2) An extremely large cricket

CROMER *n.* :
Artisan metal finisher

CROPREDY *n.* :
(arch.) Primitive term, dating from before the invention of writing, meaning autumn

CROSSAPOLL *n.* :
Internet 'dating service' for parrot breeders' parrots

CROWIE *adj.* :
Boastful

CRUCKMEOLE *interj.* :
Touchingly rustic expression of surprise

DANBY WISKE *n.* :
Advocaat-based cocktail including a lot of beaten egg-white and other alcoholic and vegetable substances

DAGENHAM *n.* :
Heavily smoked Swedish pork product

DALLINGHOO *interog.* :
First question on a BT operator's script when dealing with a 'number unobtainable' query

DAMGATE *n.* :
Field closure with severely rusted hinges

DANDERHALL *n.* :
Public Health worker's slang for a property infested with cats

DAVIDSTOW *n.* :
Condition similar to white-finger where the sufferer's foot has been subject to prolonged heavy vibration, resulting in tingling, numbness and whitening of the toes, especially in cold weather. The name is said to be due to the affected toes resembling those on the marble foot

of Michelangelo's *David*. Fortunately the coastal community of Davidswick was claimed by the North Sea long before this book was prepared (and so will not be found on the OS and require explanation)

DEARHAM *n.* :
Jamón Ibérico de Bellota

DELVINE *adj.* :
Associated with digging or rummaging (e.g. Having completed his delvine research…)

DEN OF LINDORES *n.* :
Private premises in which chocoholics can indulge their cravings excessively without censure or criticism

DERBY *n.* :
Town named solely with the purpose of frustrating those whose first language is not English

DEVONPORT *n.* :
A bold but ill-starred initiative by the English wine making industry

DIAL POST *n.* :
Device intended to confuse German invaders during WW2. Looking like a traditional British finger-post, it had a rotating post driven by a small gearbox near its base. The intention was that resistance fighters would creep out at dead of night

equipped with windlasses and rotate the signs to point in random directions

DIRT POT *n.* :
(arch.) Dialect term from North East England for a chamber pot. Due to its association with children's 'potties' it became, for a while, a common affectionate nick-name for a very young child

DOBWALLS *n.* :
(arch.) A local Cornish expression, no longer heard, referring to wattle-and-daub structures

DOWN AMPNEY *n.* :
Label frequently found adjacent to control knobs on small generator-sets manufactured in low labour-cost countries (meaning uncertain)

DOWNHILL *n.* :
Settlement named by its residents (who must surely have been unreasonably optimistic) in apparent denial of the fact that it must be uphill on the way back (qv. Uphill, is there a regional characteristic displayed here?)

DOWNLEY *adj.* :
In the direction of the resultant of all of the forces of gravity acting at a point

DRUMLEANING *n.* :
Common affliction of life-long marching-band bass drum players. Obvious visible symptoms include a

pronounced forward stoop and a tendency to hold the hands at roughly the level of the diaphragm, even when standing still. These will normally be associated with pain due to the compression of discs between the thoracic vertebrae. Sometimes informally referred to amongst medical practitioners as 'Drummer's Droop'

DRYBECK *n.* :
Small community which is currently seeking to change the name of their village to reflect the effects of global warming. At present, the three most popular choices for the new name are: Beckrushing, Fullbrook or Long Pond

DUDDO *n.* :
A village that owes its name to the creation of the Domesday Book. When the King's Recorder for Northumberland arrived at what was then a tiny hamlet, he asked his guide the name of the place. The guide, a native of distant Jedburgh, was uncertain and said so. Unfortunately he had a streaming cold. Notwithstanding, his reply was recorded and remains the place-name to this day

DUMPTON *v.* :
Made a convenience of

DUNCHURCH *n.* :
That time on a Sunday after which one may enjoy oneself

DUNGENESS *adj.* :
Empirical measure of the vileness of a dungeon cell (e.g. '... he was flung into a pit of the grossest dungeness...)

DUNMOW *n.* :
The one in a group whose experiences, escapades and adventures always exceed those of everyone else

DUNSTABLE *interj.* :
Terse but heartfelt cry of Hercules on completing the fifth of his labours

DUNNICHEN *n.* :
Registered trade name of a proprietary antihistamine cream

DUSTON *n.* :
An unloved and uncared-for ornament or memento

E

EALING *v.* :
(1) That which happens in Orspital – often; (2) A biblical miracle achieved by the Layin on of Ands

EARLEY *adj.* :
Having ideas above one's station (N.B. While it is perfectly possible for earls to have ideas above their station – as many a king will attest – this mildly derogatory term cannot meaningfully be applied to them)

EARLS COMMON *interj.* :
In the early 12th century King Stephen sought to reward his supporters by offering them newly created earldoms. These 'upstarts' were strongly despised and resented by the broadly conservative populace and the subsequent decision of Stephen's successor, Henry II, to reduce the number and power of the earls was generally popular with the people. At one of the last public ceremonies in which Stephen's full count of earls was present, it was widely reported that an urchin in the crowd, during a momentary silence, bawled the opinion "Earls! Common!" a chant quickly taken up by the crowd, much to the discomfiture of the earls. (Though widely reported,

the reader should consider that it is remarkably similar to the tale of 'The Emperor's New Clothes' and may be apocryphal. Ed.)

EASENHALL *n.* :
A notably large and well-appointed public convenience

ELFHILL *n.* :
A mound of loose friable mud caused by elves digging out their nests below (often mistaken for ant-hills)

EMNETH HUNGATE *n.* :
At the turn of the 20th century two sisters, Ethel and Emily Pancreas, who were staunch and vocal supporters of the Suffragette movement, lived in a small Norfolk village. As was common they received much ribald and critical comment from the men of the community. One evening during a particularly boisterous session in the village pub a local farmer announced that he was going to grub up a length of hedge and replace it with a 'field-gate' and that he would "like to see any of those noisy women do real work like that!" During the night that is exactly what Ethel and Emily did (it is not clear whether they actually received any assistance – they never said so). The story made the local paper and thence to the national dailies. Seeking to cover their embarrassment with a veneer of enthusiastic support, the (all male) parish council elected to rename the village in their honour

ENDON *adj.* :
Not sideways

ENSAY *v.& interj* :
(1) An unnecessarily baroque verbal embellishment supposedly to emphasise the sense when 'say' is used as a transitive verb; (2) 'cluck, cluck'

EWELL *interrog.* :
Friendly informal greeting

EWSHOT *interrog.* :
The final line, eventually cut from the film *Butch Cassidy and the Sundance Kid*

EXBOURNE *adj.* :
Post-natal

EXTED *n.* :
Discarded cuddly toy

EYAM *v.* :
When travelling in Derbyshire in 1631, René Descartes passed through Eyam causing him to remark "Eythink therefore Eyam", ridiculing the affected speech of his English hosts. A great deal too much has since been read into this whimsical remark

F

FADDILEY *adv.* :
To pick and choose in so unreasonable a way as to cause everyone around to grind their teeth in frustration

FAIRLIE *adj.* :
A bit less than very

FAIRY CROSS *n.* :
Meeting place for 'alternative' fairies

FALA *n.* :
Cheerful song, sung quietly to oneself on completion of an unpleasant task (e.g. completing a tax return)

FALA DAM *n.* :
Cheerful song, sung quietly to one's self on completion of an unpleasant task (e.g. completing a tax return) – followed by the discovery that you still have the Capital Gains section left to do

FALMER *n.* :
One who owns or runs falm (or similar lustic enterprise)

FANMORE *interj.* :
One of just two expressions used by the British in India to regulate their relationship with their punkah-wallahs

FARMOOR *adj.* :
Considerably in excess

FARTHINGHOE *interj.* :
The cry of a successful mudlark (often holding the coin aloft as proof)

FARTOWN *v.* :
To admit to breaking wind

FELIXSTOWE *n.* :
Suffolk dialect word meaning a cat's claw

FELTWELL *adj.* :
Not feeling too good now

FERNESS *adj.* :
Measurement of remoteness

FFOREST *n.* :
A p-place f-full of t-trees

FIELD BROUGHTON *adj.* :
Mandatory in-store food label for crops (such as rhubarb or asparagus) which have been grown out-of-doors, but 'forced' by being covered with black polythene sheeting (as opposed to, for example, 'free-range' rhubarb or 'barn-reared' asparagus)

FILGRAVE *n.* :

Material used to back-fill a grave once the coffin is in place. This generally comprises most of the earth originally dug out less the volume of the coffin. The excess material is most commonly the top-soil component of the spoil, which is sold on to gardeners by the sexton as his 'perk'. In old graveyards this can be particularly fertile soil

FINNART *n.* :

Art intended for aesthetic appreciation rather than practical purpose, depicting fish

FLITWICK *n.* :

Early 20th century domestic fly-killing system which released into the air a steady stream of chemical vapour (usually DDT) from a reservoir, evaporated from a wick. There is no scientific evidence to determine whether this did more damage to the flies or the people round about. (You need to be very old to understand this one!)

FLECKNOE *interj.* :

A restrained but emphatic refusal

FOBBING *v.* :

(criminal slang) Originally, removing a pocket-watch by a pickpocket. As pocket-watches became less popular it has come to mean the removal of any valuable from a fob-pocket and is regarded as one of the more skilled 'moves'

FORNIGHTY *n.* :
A category of mass-produced trimming intended for attachment to women's nightwear and lingerie

FORSINARD *v.* :
To drive-home or insert with considerable determination (I remember once watching a caretaker putting in screws with a hammer – he knew what it meant. Ed.)

G

GAYDON *n.* :
(1) A happy Mafioso; (2) A homosexual Mafioso; (3) A happy homosexual Mafioso

GELLYBURN *n.* :
(late 19th cent. criminal slang) Disfiguring condition afflicting petermen who stood too close to the safes they were blowing

GLENDUCKIE *n.* :
Scottish glen and loch famous amongst ornithologists for migratory wildfowl (N.B. not as famous as its nearby neighbour Gleneagles)

GLENGOLLY *n.* :
Small community in the far north-east of Scotland, waiting in dread for the Political Correctness police to discover them and insist they change their name

GLENVERRAGILL *n.* :
Scottish glen, just down the road from Glenslightlygill

GNOSALL *n.* :
Staffordshire dialect term for someone who thinks they know everything

GRAYS *n.* :
The portmanteau term for one of the faintest colours of the rainbow. With the latest precision prisms combined and digital enhancement, it has been shown to comprise at least fifty discrete wavelengths

GREAT BILLING *interj.* :
Brief but heartfelt congratulations telegram sent in 1967 (the early days of commercial computing) by the Minister of Power to the Head of the Gas Board. It was on the occasion that the Board's computer, after three-and-a-half years of operation, had produced its first run of invoices without one with a preposterously inflated total. A week later a popular television programme revealed each of the 35,000 invoice recipients had been notified that they were in credit to the sum of £1-10s-6½d

GREAT HECK *interj.* :
An expletive found in the manuscript of Enid Blyton's last unpublished novel *Famous Five – The Adolescent Years*. Though finished, this book was never published, being judged to have 'unsuitable content'

GREAT LUMLEY *n.* :
I can do no more than agree – and sigh

GREAT SNORING *interj.* :
The least likely compliment anyone is likely to be paid

GREATSTONE-ON-SEA *n.* :
The source of a very large wave. An early presentation on this subject to the Royal Institution led to Day and Ward's hypothesis that an eruption of the Cumbre Vieja volcano in the Canary Islands could result in a landslip and consequent tsunami that would overwhelm the Eastern Seaboard of the USA

GREENHILL *n.* :
Name of a place that is found at least four times in the UK. It is thought, in fact, to be a mirage, not only because of its multiple occurrences but also because it is invariably far away

GREENLOANING *v. n.* :
Investing in environmentally sound funds/projects

GRIMPO *n.* :
One of the traditional face designs of circus clowns

GUTCHER *interj.* :
Arguably, the Edinburgh Town Guard was one of the earliest civil order forces in the UK (even though one of the Captains of the Guard was lynched for the supposed killing of innocent civilians). They were followed shortly by the Bow Street Runners and then the Glasgow Police. Even then there was a different arrest procedure between the English and Scottish forces. In England the 'Peeler' had simply to grab a felon's collar and utter the mantra "You're collared mate" – at which

point the miscreant would submit and be led off meekly. In Scotland the phrase required to induce such quiescence was "Gutcher". Whether either of these 'verbal charms' was in the slightest effective has been open to question ever since

H

HABBERLY *adv.* :
Joyfully. (N.B. The current place name is in fact a modern abbreviation of the medieval, Habberley-Hever-Rafter, the name bestowed when the Boleyn [originally Bullen] family purchased the roof-timbers for their castle near Edenbridge from the community)

HADLEY WOOD *n.* :
A widely held belief that Hadley has always strenuously denied

HAKIN *v.* :
Suffering with a bad cough

HAMBLE-LE-RICE *v.* :
Unnecessarily arcane instruction in a cookery book by a well-known Michelin-starred chef, indicating that, when preparing egg fried-rice, the rice should be violently agitated as it is added to the cooking eggs in a wok (disgraceful French too)

HAMLET *n.* :
A collection of two or three houses with aspirations

HAMPRESTON *n.* :
Unsuccessful 1920's British tinned-food product which, though pre-dating Spam, lacked the effects of rationing to generate sufficient demand

HAMSTERLY *adv.* :
In the manner of a hamster (e.g. His cheeks swelled hamsterly, he approached the grind of the daily 'treadmill' hamsterly – bowel function is also commonly associated with this adverb, but politeness forbids…)

HANDY CROSS *n.* :
Crucifix fitted with a pocket-clip, belt-clip or supplied with a quick-draw holster. Intended for travellers in Transylvania

HANGING HOUGHTON *n.* :
Late 17th cent. Judge noted for the rehabilitational effectiveness of his sentencing ("Few who come before me do so again.")

HAGLEY *adj.* :
Unprepared to pay the full ticket price on anything, even if the proceeds go to charity

HAMPTON COURT *v phr.* :
Situation brought about by the careless adjustment of a zip

HARDLEY *adv.* :
With considerable force

HARDWAY *adv.* :
Reputedly, standing up in a hammock

HARPLEY *adv.* :
In a manner akin to stroking the strings of a harp (e.g. '… her fingers strayed, harpley down his chest towards the buckle of his belt… ' [with thanks probably due to Mills & Boon])

HARPOLE *n.* :
The wooden handle of a traditionally-made loo brush

HASTOE *n.* :
Name originally and wrongly ascribed to a supposed set of mammals of the group 'odd-toed ungulates' (that includes the horse) all of which support themselves on one toe. It was initially believed that they only possessed one toe until later research revealed that there were other vestigial toes, undeveloped

HATTON OF FINTRAY *n.* :
Hereditary title and privilege granted by King James I of England to his north-Scottish barber who, seeking to negotiate a better price for his work whilst shaving the King, inadvertently gave him the idea for the Great Contract. As a consequence the eldest child of the McEachern family from Aberdeen may, to this day, wear a head covering in the presence of the monarch

HAUGH OF GLASS *n.* :
A heavy breath made with an open mouth onto a mirror or pair of spectacles before polishing

HAUTES CROIX *n.* :
A seasonally produced sweet currant bun first developed by the boulanger of the eponymous settlement on Jersey in order to appeal to his predominantly English customers

HAVERCROFT *n.* :
A person who feels, and tactlessly remarks, that it is infra-dig to own a holiday home 'on the coast', 'in Spain', etc.

HAWARDEN *n.* :
Officer found in many British east-coast villages during the 18th and 19th centuries whose task was to warn local residents and inshore fishermen of impending sea-fog

HAWKEDON *v.* :
To be struck by a 'lucky' bird-dropping from a bird of prey

HAYHILLOCK *n.* :
Traditional farming term for a haystack that has been adversely affected by the weather

HEALD GREEN *adv.* :
A sure sign of incipient infection in a wound

HEDSOR *n.* :
A mild hangover

HENRYD *v.* :
Vacuumed using an industrial vacuum cleaner

HESSAY *n.* :
A piece of written work sometimes required of students at Rugby, Harrow, Eton and Winchester

HIGHTAE *n.* :
A light snack during the late afternoon

HILTON *adj.* :
Archaeological time period covering the latter part of the Stone Age. It is characterised as the period from when humans first attached handles to their tools and weapons. It marks a significant intellectual step, namely the realisation that artefacts could be assembled from two or more components rather than simply formed from a single object

HINTS *n.* :
Most often delivered too late and a waste of time anyway

HISTON *n.* :
A poorly fitting piston on a steam locomotive

HOLE *n.* :
A community apparently not much liked by its inhabitants

HOLLEE *n.*:
Place said to have inspired, or be the birthplace of, the traditional Sans Carol ('Now the holly bears a berry...')

HOLLOWELL *n.*:
Statement of the obvious

HOPTON WAFERS *n.*:
Biscuit baked without shortening or fat and relying on a mono-pedal treading technique (now largely lost due to mechanisation) for its thin, hard texture

HORNING *v.*:
The head-butting activity carried out by elks and similar animals during the rut

HORRA *n.*:
A hideous, ravening, amphibious sea monster of myth common to the Shetlands and coastal Norway. The Lerwick Horra is reputed to come ashore on stormy nights and carry off tax inspectors and other government officials

HORSHAM *n.*:
Economy pre-packed supermarket cold meat of questionable provenance

HURTISO *interj.*:
Childish 'pidgin' expression for 'it is very painful'

HUTTON ROOF *n.*:
A poorly constructed loft extension

HUGGATE *adj. & n.* :
(1) In a manner involving an embrace (e.g. … grasped in a huggate grip…); (2) A person or thing embraced (e.g. …the huggates were then required to stand in line until she left…)

I

ICKLEFORD *n.*:
The Ka

IFFLEY *adv.*:
Somewhat doubtfully

ILLEY *n.*:
Alternative excuse for a day off if you think your boss is getting suspicious of your 'sickies'

INCHBARE *n.*:
The gap that opens up between the top of the sock and the bottom of the trouser-leg when seated

INGOE *v.*:
(arch.) 14th cent. expression 'to enter'

INNERLEVEN *n.*:
Regular member of a football team

INSKIP *adj.*:
Discarded

IPSWICH *n.*:
Device to hide the identity of a computer which is being used for nefarious purposes

J

JOCKEY END *n.* :
Damage to the sacral nerves or lumbar disks which is an occupational hazard for professional horse-riders

K

KEEVIL *n.*:
Unit of measure used predominantly by anglers, equals one thousand weevils

KENLEY *adv.*:
Knowingly

KENMORE *n.*:
A particularly well-informed person

KERSHADER *n.*:
A handkerchief knotted to form a head covering

KETTLESING *v.*:
To make a quiet warbling whining-noise when unhappy

KIDWELLY *n.*:
Child's boot

KILBERRY *n.*:
Old country name for the fruit of the Yew (N.B. the seed is more poisonous)

KILBRIDE *n.*:
One of the seven classic plots for murder mystery stories (murder in the locked room, etc., etc.)

KILDARY *adj.* :
Very like Richard Chamberlain

KILNDOWN *n.* :
Major equipment failure in a pottery

KILLEARN *n.* :
The study or practice of assassination

KINLOSS *v.* :
Missing far-away relatives

KNIGHTON WOODS *n.* :
The House of Lords Bowls Club

L

LACOCK *n.* :
Unofficial French national emblem

LAMBDEN *n.* :
Playhouse for young sheep

LAMLASH *n.* :
Item of shepherd's equipment

LAMPETER *n.* :
Type of variety act in which the performer appears to eat razor blades, light bulbs, telephone directories and such

LANARK *n.* :
French police informer

LANCASTER *n.* :
A designer and installer of home computer networks

LANDRAKE *n.* :
Early form of horse-drawn harrow

LANGLEE *n.* :
The feeling experienced by a household's

nominated 'IT expert' when an Internet connection is re-established after a fraught period of outage.

LARGIEMORE *interj.* :
Make it bigger

LATHERON *v.* :
To apply shaving soap too generously

LATHERONWHEEL *n.* :
Electric 'beauty' product to automatically apply 'a generous quantity of luxurious, nutrient-rich shaving foam' – with any number of suggested cosmetic benefits

LAUNCELLS *n.* :
Individual pieces of turf

LAXO *n.* :
Stuffing mix for particularly tight-arsed chickens and ducks

LE BIGARD *?.* :
No. Can't think of one for that

LEAP CROSS *n.* :
Medieval predecessor to Free Running

LEAVELAND *v.* :
To set sail

LENTON *v.* :
(1) Used for support; (2) Coerced

LETCHWORTH *n.*:
Notably attractive and provocatively dressed young person

LETTEREWE *n.*:
(arch.) Sheep trained to collect newspapers, letters, etc. and deliver them to the shepherd. This was a technique used by fell shepherds to motivate lazy and slow-learning sheepdogs

LETTON *n.*:
Someone who cannot keep a secret

LEWDOWN *n.*:
Habit held to be the mark of a gentleman

LEYTON *n.*:
A TV programme you have set to record which does not start on time "…because of our extended coverage of… ", so that you miss the last enthralling fifteen minutes

LICKEY END *n.*:
That part of an ice-lolly which at any point during its consumption is farthest from the stick

LIGHTWATER *n.*:
Water comprising two oxygen atoms and one atom of the theoretical hydrogen isotope Nullium (in which both the neutron and proton have been removed from the nucleus). Relying on the precise manipulation of the electron spin to exactly balance

the forces in the electron-shell when the nucleus is removed, thus avoiding atomic collapse, this material has never been produced in practice. During WW2, both sides' atomic-bomb programmes expended considerable effort to develop Lightwater believing it would be easier and cheaper to transport in large quantities to the point of use where it could be reconstituted first into 'normal' and then 'heavy' water

LIPHOOK *n.* :
(1) Basic item of angling equipment; (2) Body piercing accessory used to connect the upper lip to the outside edge of one of the nostrils or the nasal septum

LITTLE ONN *n.* :
Staffordshire dialect expression for an idle person or wastrel

LITTLE WEIGHTON *n.* :
First sign of a failing diet

LITTLEMORE *interj.* :
Second sign of a failing diet

LLANDOGGET *n.* :
A tolerant location in Wales popular with amorous exhibitionists

LLANFYLLIN *v.* :
Welsh term for the managed on-shore dumping of rubbish

LLANGROVE *n.* :
Shoreline area of brackish swampy water supporting partly submerged trees between Cardiff and Llantwit Major – has never developed enough to become famous due to the scouring effect of the Severn bore

LLANGUA *n.* :
The line '…wound my heart with a monotonous Llangua… ', from Paul Verlaine's poem, 'Chanson d'automne' is famous for being a code phrase sent to the French Resistance signalling the start of the Normandy Invasion. Though proud of their place in history, the people of Llangua insist that their community is more interesting than Verlaine's work implies

LLANSPYDDID *v.* :
Admission of a dyslexic network hacker

LOCHEE *n.* :
One significantly inconvenienced by a security device

LOCKING STUMPS *n.* :
Device used for match fixing in cricket

LOFTHOUSE *n.* :
Studio apartment

LOLWORTH *adj.* :
A measure of how funny (or otherwise) a joke may

be (e.g. ...a repost of great lolworth...)

LONG EATON *adj.* :
(1) A meal taken with excruciatingly boring company; (2) One's last meal which was a long time ago

LONG LOAD *n.* :
Somerset village which has found a most effective method of promoting itself by displaying its name on the back of many articulated lorries

LONGYESTER *n.* :
(arch.) Term applied to the previous day if it was unbearably boring or fruitless

LOW BARBETH *n.* :
Liz, a dear friend of my late teens, who was a particularly accomplished Limbo dancer

LOWER ASSENDON *v.* :
To sit down

LOWER LYE *v.* :
To hide even more effectively than if one lies low

LOWER MORE *n.* :
Hand signal given by a slinger to a crane driver – often preceding the interjection, Oops!

LOWER PEOVER *interj.* :
'Mature' response to some of the more puerile

graffiti on the walls of public urinals

LOWER ROADWATER *n.* :
Somerset village where the name board only becomes visible in times of severe drought

LOWER SWELL *n.* :
A subsiding sea state

LUFNESS *n.* :
(sailing term) Measure of a vessel's ability to sail close to the wind

LYMPNE *n.* :
Medical name for the condition where one, or more, knees exhibit no patellar reflex

LYNESS *n.* :
The reciprocal of truthfulness

M

MACMERRY *n.* :
Seasonal burger promotion – often involving paper hats

MAGGOTS END *n.* :
(1) Bluebottles; (2) Fish bait

MAINSRIDDLE *n.* :
Wiring installed by an amateur electrician

MAMBLE *v.* :
To mutter incoherently, at length

MANCHESTER *n.* :
An early-Victorian device for "…exercising and developing your chest muscles discreetly in the privacy of your own home… ". Comprising a stout polished-mahogany frame, ropes, pulleys and heavy bags of sand the Manchester was anything but discreet and consequently achieved only limited sales; those sales were almost exclusively in parts of the country favoured with sandy beaches

MANDALLY *v.* :
To study, intently, something near at hand when not sure what to do next

MARKET WEIGHTON *n.* :
The non-existent 'virtual weight' of goods bought from a street trader resulting from their thumb accidentally resting on the back of the scale-pan

MARKINCH *n.* :
Technical term for the indented graduations on a steel rule

MARLCLIFF *n.* :
A huge pile of natural soil conditioner

MARLOW BOTTOM *n.* :
A disrespectful nickname for a woman of middle years or older with short legs

MARSH GIBBON *n.* :
Small, shy, migratory bird which, due to its hooting cry was, until recent sightings, believed to be an escaped ape

MARTOCK *n.* :
(arch.) Old West Country name for what would now be called a grandmother clock

MARTYR WORTHY *adj.* :
One who, by popular acclaim (possibly mistaken), the world would be better off without

MARYPORT *n.* :
Small access hatch near the waterline in the stern of a square-rigged sailing ship. Actually intended

to allow access to the rudder pintles (hinges) whilst at sea, their name derives from the fact that they were an ideal means of introducing ladies-of-the-town to a vessel, unseen, whilst in harbour

MATCHING GREEN *n.* **:**
An Essex village, twinned with Olive Green (qv.) having, in a misguided moment, purchased a significant quantity of Olive Green's surplus paint stock

MATLOCK *n.* **:**
Small fittings (usually plastic press-stud or toggle devices) attached to floor-covering to keep it in place. Most commonly found in cars

MATLOCK BATH *n.* **:**
Modern style of bath with 'built-in' Matlock (qv.) fixings to prevent compatible bath mats from skittering dangerously across the floor as an unwary bather exits the tub

MEATHOP *n.* **:**
An entertainment briefly 'popular' during WW2. It was a public dance differing from the usual 'hop' by the serving of fresh meat as the interval refreshments. It was generally considered 'bad form' to speculate about the nature or source of the meat. In this case, 'popular' meant 'sought-after' rather than 'widely attended'. The right contacts and 'a few bob' were prerequisites to get tickets

MERE BROW *adj.* :
Even less sophisticated and cultured than 'low-brow', scarcely 'brow' at all

MERIDEN *n.* :
A secluded hideaway where children of previous generations would engage in cheerful japes and high jinks. Now an unsavoury spot watched carefully by the police

MID LAVANT *n.* :
From the late 11th century to well into the 16th century, castles and manor houses would regularly employ large numbers of servants to carry out the day-to-day running of the establishment. Those employed in the laundry were known as lavants. In very large and wealthy households, teams of specialist lavants were formed to develop and hand down the skills necessary to deal with different types of washing. Mid-lavants would handle the washing of day-to-day attire, made of hard-wearing materials, Cool-lavants would deal with wool, lace and delicate items, while Hot-lavants would wash whites and colourfast cottons. It is said that the Beauchamp family employed an experimental lavant to stand on the battlements of Worcester Castle whirling washed items round and round over his head to shake off surplus water. This experiment was soon abandoned with the widespread introduction of the mangle

MIDDLE WALLOP *n.* :
In boxing a high-scoring but technically difficult punch delivered below the opponent's diaphragm but above the belt

MIDDLETOWN *n.* :
A thoroughly pleasant but unremarkable place with no significant up-town or down-town areas. The community is generally very pleased that the village is called Middletown, of which there is only one in the UK, rather than Middleton, of which there are more than thirty (royal and peri-royal personages excepted)

MIDGLEY *adv.* :
In the manner of a gnat or similar small insect, able to hover and then instantly and seemingly effortlessly move swiftly in any direction (e.g. Claudia hesitated, midgley, near the door)

MILL MEECE *n.* :
Small rodents regularly found in flour mills. Though of little consequence to anyone except the miller they have nonetheless achieved almost unparalleled stardom for centuries, through poems, songs, stories, films, in fact almost every form of popular entertainment

MOCKBEGGAR *n.* :
A thoroughly disgraceful game popular in South East England during the Middle Ages. Played by most of the population of two or more

neighbouring villages the objective was to hound a beggar out of your own village and into your neighbour's whilst the neighbouring villagers defended and tried to drive him or her back. The 'game' was played with only one beggar at a time. Virtually any method of hounding was deemed 'fair': insults, curses, blows, beating, stoning (generally with clods of earth to prolong the 'fun'), buckets of cold water, setting light to the clothes. Extraordinarily, the use of animals, such as savaging by dogs, and the wielding of professionally made weapons was not permitted. The losing village had to provide a beggar for the next scheduled match. Beggars were not permitted to be entered for more than one match. Unwary beggars inadvertently straying into the area might well find themselves the object of a scratch match, or else being detained, fed and trained up to give 'his/her' side a clear advantage at the next scheduled match. Seeking to civilise their parishioners, local clergy banded together to declare that playing the game was a sin and introduced their flocks to a gentler game of cards. It is not surprising that this game has become known as Beggar-my-Neighbour, Strip-Jack-Naked or Beat-Your-Neighbour-Out-of-Doors

MONEYDIE *n.* :
Tool for stamping out coins (that is, producing them, not doing away with them)

MONIMAIL *n.* :
A short-lived successor to the postal order

MONKHOPTON *n.* :
A frequent cart (latterly, bus) service between a monastery and the centre of the nearest town or village

MONKSEATON *n.* :
Derogatory term for the misericord, widespread amongst the laity who felt that monks were trying to deceive them, pretending to stand, piously, throughout a service when, in fact they were not

MORANGIE *adj.* :
A bit like a meringue

MUDFORD SOCK *n.* :
A mishap that can befall anyone taking part in an Iron-man competition, after which they must compete barefoot

N

NAAST *n.* :
A particularly villainous character in a film, TV programme or book. A naast should not be confused with a 'baddie' who may do anti-social things and be a bit naughty but, it will turn out, has very likely: been starved of affection when young, come from a broken home, always looked up to his older (naughtier) sibling, wanted to get his dear old mum the things she never had, or even, absent-mindedly, simply put on a black hat by mistake when leaving home that morning. If a baddie does anything seriously wrong it will surely be under the guidance of a naast. A naast, on the other hand, will not only be evil but will gloat and glory in his/her wickedness. Baddies will eventually (and inevitably) fail a naast but experienced naasts will expect this – and have A PLAN. We must always hope our hero is one step ahead

NANPANTAN *n.* :
DIY tanning cream made to granny's own recipe. The basic formula, common to all variants, comprises meat browning from the bottom of the roasting tin and moisturising cream. Other

constituents vary depending on whose granny it is. Granny will assure any doubting potential users that it worked very well for her when she was a girl and was particularly popular in the '30s – although it did attract the flies a bit. For most people the use of nanpantan ended in 1949 when clothes rationing ended before meat rationing

NANTYGLO *n.* :
A simple shelter made of snow by Welsh hill farmers tending their flocks during the most severe winters. As a safety precaution such shelters were usually constructed beside a stream or brook (hence the prefix nant-). If the snow had thawed enough to see that the stream was flowing, it was time to leave before the structure collapsed on you

NEEDHAM MARKET *n.* :
Slang name given by locals in London's East End to the first totally kosher street market established there in the late 18th century. The name was not seen as derogatory and was used by gentiles and Jews alike

NEAR SAWREY *adj.* :
Of a location close to where wood cutting is in progress

NESSCLIFFE *n.* :
Correct technical term for a large pile of bulk instant coffee granules immediately before packaging and dispatch

NESTON *n.* :
Large rectangular chimney found on many old houses in central and northern Europe, popular as roosts for storks

NETHER CRIMMOND *n.* :
The base part to the most popular setting of 'The Lord's my Shepherd'

NETHER MOOR *interj.* :
Cry peculiar to ravens that are hard-of-hearing

NETHER WALLOP *n.* :
In boxing, now outlawed by the introduction of the Marquis of Queensberry rules in the 1860s, a blow delivered below the opponent's belt, usually to devastating effect, much used in bare-knuckle bouts

NETHERPLACE *n.* :
A rather coy term for Hell, first used by rather coy Victorians

NETHERTHONG *n.* :
The correct term for the garment that is now called a thong. The abbreviation 'thong' is imprecise and has a wider meaning than that for which it is now commonly used

NETLEY *adv.* :
In the manner of a net (e.g. '... the vines enveloped the struggling creature, netley... ')

NETTLEBED *n.* :
(arch.) Traditional term invoking the mythical cause of poor sleep due to a guilty conscience (e.g. "…Squire will find that he has a nettlebed tonight. Poor Angie!")

NEW DEER *n.* :
(1) A fawn; (2) Also used briefly by a well-known paint company as the name of a sort-of-beige colour that never became very popular)

NEW EARSWICK *n.* :
One of the arsenal of alternative treatments offered by the 'health and beauty' industry is ear candling, in which a hollow candle is inserted into the ear of the subject and lit, supposedly drawing wax and debris (!) from the ear canal. During the last decade, research has documented several medical conditions consequent upon this treatment, including candle wax occlusion and local burns. There are at least two recorded instances of persons setting their houses on fire by ear candling. Several studies have concluded that the residue from the procedure left in a candle was not ear pollutants, but simply candle wax and soot. Seeking to circumvent this negative publicity, the industry has recently developed the 'New Earswick'. This is a self-supporting highly absorbent wick impregnated with a minimal amount of combustion accelerant. The wick is placed in the ear and lit. A brief flame sears down the wick generating just enough heat to melt the

ear wax which rises up the wick and burns off as fuel. Supposedly there is no residue – even the subject's ear one imagines. (From the author's research on this subject he is strongly of the opinion that these therapies should be avoided. Ed.)

NEW INVENTION *n.* :
Tautological term for an item (usually a product or process). The term was created by the Marketing Industry exclusively for use by the Marketing Industry. The rest of us make do with 'new' or 'invention'

NEW LEAKE *n.* :
(1) Good news for a farmer; (2) Bad news for a sea-captain (a bit like red skies, really. Ed.)

NEWBURY *interj.* :
The traditional cry of a player of Bury St Edmunds (qv.) who, having won the last round, has succeeded in hiding (troving) a new 'disappeared' (game term for a search object) and that the next round may now commence.

NEWDIGATE *n.* :
As the craze for naturism spread out from its early avant-garde adherents in London, this term for the entrance to a naturist colony was first recorded in Surrey. It briefly spread but then vanished as the whole idea became rather 'yesterday' and boring

NEWLANDRIG *n.*:
The equipment on a recently announced site for an exploratory fracking borehole

NEWTON ROW *n.*:
A long-standing but simmering legal dispute between the more-than seventy-five communities in the UK bearing the name Newton, regarding the hierarchy of precedence accorded by the date of their foundation

NEWTYLE *n.*:
A Scottish hat-making community that decided in the mid-19th century to change its name to promote its product. Sadly the marketing consultant responsible for the community's re-branding was not an 'East Ender' by birth and so did not realise that the reference was not rhyming slang but just a simple allusion and thus should keep the standard spelling of 'tile'

NINEVEH *n.*:
Community once famed for the building of quinquiremes. Long since land-locked, all evidence of this skilled trade is now long gone

NO MAN'S HEATH *n.*:
Sizeable area, once common land, that is now a barren landscape, pitted with large craters and the blackened, twisted stumps of trees. As this is in the UK, no plausible explanation has yet been advanced for its existence

NOBOTTLE *n.* :
One who, no matter how serious the fault or how grievous the wrong, always insists that they "can't be bothered" to complain

NORTON *n.* :
Northamptonshire dialect term for a nudist

NOTTAGE *n.* :
The skill of effectively joining pieces of: string, cord, rope, vine, etc. (e.g. '…the Scoutmaster had a Leaping Wolf and both the Nottage and Advanced Nottage badges… ' quote from the story by Conan Doyle, 'The Case of the Strained Woggle'. Ed.)

OAKAMOOR *n.* :
The love of an oak tree

OCCOLD *n.* :
The first and overwhelming thought to fill the mind when entering a swimming pool

ODSTOCK *n.* :
The apparent stocking policy of the new generation of cut-price supermarkets

OFFCHURCH *adj.* :
State caused by the onset of atheism, a dislike of the new vicar or manifest favouritism with the flower rota

OGLE *v.* :
To gaze in a politically incorrect fashion, usually whilst harbouring politically incorrect thoughts.

OGLET *n.* :
A sly ogle (qv.)

OLD DAILLY *n.* :
Yesterday's news

OLDLANGHO *n.* :
Released in 1959 amid the vogue for producing 'pop' versions of classical and well-known tunes, this rock-a-billy version of 'Auld Lang Syne' sank without trace

OLD NEWTON *n.* :
Though somewhat self-contradictory this name was wisely adopted by the community's residents many years ago, thereby removing themselves from all the costs, aggravations and frustrations of involvement in the Newton Row (qv.). The inclusion of the preceding 'Old' was doubly clever in that it tends to cause a supposition of seniority regardless of the eventual outcome of the Newton Row

OLIVE GREEN *n.* :
Village in the Trent Valley, so named after the predominant colour of its public structures, street-furniture and buildings. This is the result of the Parish Council mistakenly buying 50,000 gallons of ex-WD surplus paint after the Second World War. The possibility of a name change is not forecast until 2150

ONGAR *interj.* :
Customary salutation at the start of a duel-by-swords made by a duellist whose opponent is a bit quick off the mark

ONICH *n.* :
The spot where Dunnichen (qv.) should be applied

OTHERY *adj.* :
Object so amazingly like something else it could easily be mistaken. Recently, the term is becoming used in connection with similar looking people e.g. "Fred and Joe; now there's an othery pair!"). **Note:** linguistic purists maintain that it *is* permissible to use the word without defining the object to which the subject is similar; in common usage the omission of the reference object is taken to imply that the subject is nondescript (e.g. "Oh, he's a bit too othery!")

OUGHTERSIDE *n.* :
The side of an object which the inner side is within

OXLODE *n.* :
Reputedly very good for the roses

P

PABAIL *v.* :
Arrange a suspect's release from prison

PAINTER'S FORSTAL *n.* :
(1, of artists) Low table or small stool placed in front of the subject when painting 'life portraits'. Plants or other objects would be placed on the forstal obscuring the view of those parts of the subject that were deemed politically incorrect (for their time) or, just simply thoroughly unsightly; (2, of decorators) Ruse used to prevent actionable accidents when painting upper storeys outside. The oldest and simplest recorded was a sign, attached to the decorator's ladder, saying 'This Ladder is Unlucky'. As superstition dwindled a new generation of signs such as 'Decorator Carries an Adrenaline EpiPen', have been introduced

PAINURE *n.* :
Being in a condition of pain – can reflect both duration and intensity (e.g. "… of course, after that, he had a most terrible painure. Frankly, I think she should be ashamed of herself.")

PANBRIDE *n.* :
A woman married principally for her ability as a housekeeper. (NB. Panhusband and Panpartner are anticipated in the next edition of this book. Ed.)

PANT GLAS *v.& n.* :
(1) To breathe heavily on a rarely used glass before rubbing with a cloth when an unexpected visitor arrives; (2) Mirror in an Ann Summers shop

PARBOLD *adj.* :
A person who is bit 'mouthy', but not really brave

PATRICROFT *v.* :
To consign one's father, against their will, to life in a small cottage in the north of Scotland

PAUPERHAUGH *n.* :
Deep and disparaging sigh given by a 'toff' or opinionated person with money when confronted with a *Big Issue* seller

PECKET WELL *interj.* :
Mantra 'chanted' by all mother birds to their young when feeding. Recent research suggests that this behaviour is genetic in origin and that interspecies transfer introduced it to the human genome during the time of the Neanderthals. Many people say that they recognise resonances of it in their own childhood

PEGWELL *interj.* :
Sound domestic advice for a windy day

PEN-Y-FELIN *interj.* :
Phrase grizzled by more than a few young children whose pocket money has accidentally entered the drainage system

PENDOCK *n.* :
Heavily-weighted object equipped with a 'holster' to hold a writing instrument attached to it by chain. Commonly found in banks and similar premises

PENISTONE *n.* :
(1) A rocky outcrop which if viewed at just the right angle at sunrise on mid-summer's day presents an uncanny resemblance to the silhouette of William Penn (1644-1718), founder of Pennsylvania. The popularity of this tourist attraction has dwindled steadily over the last 400 years. (2) An unfortunately phallic graveyard obelisk

PENKRIDGE *n.* :
The ridge of a roof decorated with ornamental tiles. Popular on mid-late Victorian villas, by far the most common design gave the roof a spine punctured with equi-spaced holes, making it look as though it should be attached to a spiral binder. Invariably the gable-ends of such roofs were completed with an end piece usually in the form

of a dragon's head or a curly knob. These were intended to attest to the designer's high aesthetic sensibilities

PENKILL *n.* :
Tangible evidence suggesting that the pen, perhaps, may be mightier than the sword

PENMARK *n.* :
As often as not, something you hope will come out in the wash

PENMORFA *n.* :
Novelty writing instrument that can also be used as a torch, screwdriver, toothpick and oyster-knife

PENNY MOOR *interj.* :
High-risk gambit only employed by *brave* children collecting money with a traditional Guy, in early November. Often immediately precedes a traditional threat response of "…get a good clip round the ear!"

PENSELWOOD *n.* :
Tree of the Yew family which, if skilfully coppiced, produces multiple slender, resilient, straight-grained stems used for nearly two centuries for the manufacture of traditional writing instruments. The advent of the modern pencil – all too often made of ground-up plastic drinking cups – has largely wiped out the plant and its husbandry

PENTREFELIN *v.* :
The act of harvesting the stems of the Penselwood tree (qv.). This is a process of considerable skill; the harvester needing to remove the mature stems whilst leaving the 'whips' for next year's growth intact

PENYGROES *n.* :
(arch.) Popular informal name for individual accounts in early Friendly Societies, Mutuals and Building Societies

PERCYHORNER *n.* :
Jack's brother, who tended not to use his *thumb* when eating pie

PERIVALE *n.* :
The high ground surrounding a valley

PETER'S MARLAND *n.* :
The part of the country that Peter's mother comes from

PETTYCUR *n.* :
Small lap-dog

PICTON *n.* :
The least popular child in the class

PINNER *n.* :
The correct title for the Senior Curator of the Lepidoptera collection of the British Museum

PLESHEY *adj.* :
(of a surface) Like a swamp, marsh or mire

PLUNGAR *n.* :
A sink unblocker specifically made for the Essex DIY market

PLWMP *n.* :
The noise made when a large spoonful of porridge falls on a feather pillow or cushion

POLPERRO *n.* :
A class of show-parrot bred to have black and white plumage in a diamond pattern and a black bar across the eyes

POLSHAM *n.* :
A budgerigar trying to imitate a parrot

POLING CORNER *n.* :
The little hutch you go into to mark a ballot paper

POLYPHANT *n.* :
Cat sized Palaeocene pachyderm with the earliest known evidence of proboscid development. Recent advances in the X-ray photography of fossil remains show it to have had clawed feet and multi-coloured feathers

PONTWELLY *n.* :
A small Welsh community which, unable to afford to build a bridge, requires its residents to

wear boots to cross the brook which divides the hamlet

PORTINNISHERRICH *interj.* :
Phonetic spelling of a comment that might well be passed by a portmeirion (qv.) dinner guest to his neighbour on noticing the host accidentally pouring a new bottle of port into the wrong decanter

PORTMEIRION *adj.* :
The state of dinner-party guests once the decanter has circulated three or four times

POTTERS CROUCH *n.* :
Painful lower-back problem resulting from muscle spasm and tendon inflammation in that area. Named after its most common sufferers, this condition is very frequently exhibited by: potters spending too long over their wheel without a break, gardeners spending too long over their potting benches without a break (also, crouchers spending too long over their pot without a break – but this is usually dismissed)

PRESTATYN *n.* :
(1) Mild cholesterol-limiting medication offered, with dietary advice, to individuals showing the first signs of raised lipid levels; (2) A gentleman's opera hat

PRESTWICK *n.* :
Painful medical condition caused by the regular wearing of tight underpants

PWLL TRAP *n.* :
Mechanical device used in the early stages of processing wool. Essentially a very coarse carding comb the pwll trap removes burrs, intractable knots (pwlls) and other unwanted hard lumps from the wool. Also used in the production of 'budget' sheepskins

PYE CORNER *n.* :
Secluded nook where Percyhorner (qv.) used to retire to enjoy his pies

Q

QUADRING *n*. :
Four-burner cooking hob

QUEENZIEBURN *interj*. :
Entry from the exclusive childcare manual *Ye Guidanse for Royalle Nanniesse* first commissioned by Henry VIII and updated and revised in successive royal households ever since. This particular exclamation is intended to warn a young potential monarch that she is about to touch something uncomfortably hot

R

RADWINTER *n.* :
A brand of anti-freeze that is so cheap that you know it's a mistake to buy it – although you're tempted...

RAINOW *interj.* :
A 'maiden' forecast from a nervous novice weather-forecaster

RAMSNEST COMMON *n.* :
A site (then truly a common) named in the early 18th century by an unknown member of the Royal Society as an ironic salute to Olaus Magnus, Archbishop of Uppsala. Olaus (1490-1557) was a vocal proponent of the theory that swallows in northern Europe over-wintered under the ice in ponds and rivers. That idea having recently been dismissed by the Society, the unrecorded member felt the occasion should be honoured by a memorial in perpetuity. In establishing a place-name suggesting an equally preposterous natural circumstance, which has since been recorded in the OS, he undoubtedly succeeded

RANTON *v.* :
The default behaviour of the more annoying type of politician and clergyman

RATTERY *n.* :
A holiday home for pet rodents

RAWDON *v.* :
The act of a football crowd when their team has the upper hand (or probably foot) in a match

REDDING *v.* :
Blushing strongly

REDFORDGREEN *interj.* :
Sometimes found in the pace notes for a colour-blind rally driver

REISQUE *adj.* :
A bit naughty!

RESOLVEN *v.* :
Having been sorted out

REST AND BE THANKFUL *interj.* :
What meaning could possibly be better than the literal one? Possibly the finest entry in this book. I shall do so whenever opportunity permits

REYDON *v.* :
What a sun-bather hopes will happen to them (amongst other things, I daresay)

RHEINDOWN *n.* :
An arcane jargon term from the travel industry, one of two types of cruise offered on the German rivers. Downstream cruises use less fuel and, taking less time, require less food and drink when compared with the following week's upstream (Rheinup) leg. The term rarely appears in advertisements

RHOSBIERIO *n.* :
A Welsh-owned bar in Ibiza

RHOSCOLYN *n.* :
The Rhosbierio's (qv.) owner's husband

RHYD-Y-FELIN *interj.* :
It is an established part of Welsh folklore that the woodland fairy-warriors use corgis as their mounts and battle chargers. What is not yet much recorded is that, with the growth of towns, the urbanised fairies ('chavies' as they are sometimes known) have taken to riding trained feral cats. It is clear that the two groups are still struggling for supremacy and, for those sensitive enough to hear it, the chavies' battle-cry of 'Rhyd-y-Felin' ('ride-a-cat') can often be heard chiming through the night. (Mercifully, the Great Powers have not yet learned of this conflict!)

RHYND *n.* :
The outer edge of a Welsh cheese

RIBY *adj.* :
Like a Size-0 model

RICKLING *n.* :
A little Rick (e.g. one of my children)

RIDLEY *adj.* :
Enigmatic

ROADMEETINGS *n.* :
A polite term for crashes. Not yet adopted by the insurance industry, but surely it will be soon

ROADWATER *n.* :
A Somerset village that cunningly chose a name far more effective at slowing through traffic than any number of 'Please Drive Carefully through our Village' signs

ROBIN HOOD'S BAY *n.* :
The famed outlaw's favourite horse. By repute this magnificent animal was struck and killed by the first arrow released by Robin from his death-bed requiring him to fire a second shaft

ROCKEND *n.* :
The only two places on the eponymous confection where it is possible to discern what all the included lettering actually says (and then not always)

RODEN *adj.* :
(of drains, sewers, etc.) Just cleaned using a traditional bamboo rodding-tool

RODHUISH *adj.* :
(of drains, sewers, etc.) Just cleaned using a modern water-jet rodding-tool

ROGERSTONE *n.* :
One of the less common sexual variants

ROOKWITH *n.* :
Almost anything would be an improvement one imagines

ROTTINGDEAN *n.* :
An ecclesiastical officer who is probably due for replacement

ROUND SPINNEY *n.* :
Children's party game mostly involving the participants falling over – and occasionally being sick

RUBHA BAN *n.* :
Celtic for an elastic fastener

RUGELEY *adv.* :
In the manner of a mat (e.g. '...the comforting warmth of the fire with Fido lying, rugeley, in front of it...')

RUNCORN *n.* :
Small area of hardened skin on the foot caused by jogging

RUNTALEAVE *v.* :
To remove the weakest, youngest piglet from a

litter, allowing it to be hand-reared and reducing the demands on the sow

RYME INTRINSECA *n.* :
Produced in London in 1785 the *Ryme Intrinseca* was a publication prompted by the flowering of the English Romantic Poets. It was in essence a thesaurus for poets containing not only synonyms but also lists of matching rhymes cross referenced by sound and meaning, and essays on various styles of verse with meter-guides and tips for when each might be most effectively employed. The book was marketed at both 'professional' poets and aspiring amateurs with the implicit promise that, with its aid, the latter might easily become the former. Indeed, as encouragement the author included this inspirational poem on the back cover:

> *When poets stall and stumble to construct a fine quatrain*
> *They pull out Ryme Intrinseca to ease their museless pain*
> *A tome of rhymes and meanings all, of scansions, odes and stress*
> *I recommend you get it, it's the key to your success*

S

St ERNEY *n.* :
Patron saint of Premium Bond holders and milkmen

St MARGARET'S HOPE *n.* :
St Michael?

SALINE *n.* :
South African ferry company

SALTAIRE *n.* :
Ozone

SALTBURN *n.* :
Pronounced reddening of the skin accompanied by extreme local soreness and pain, followed by skin peeling. Referred to as saltburn by rugged yachting and boating 'types' to disguise the fact that they have simply been out in the sun too long without protection (which wouldn't be at all rugged)

SAND HOE *interj.* :
One of the standard lookout's cries from the days of sail. Though concerning, it generally occasioned much less panicking and rushing about than the two alternatives, "Rocks Ahead!" or "Breakers!"

SANDAL MAGNA *n.* :
Coarse volcanic ejaculate used for road-building aggregate and the manufacture of obscured glass

SANDNESS *adj.* :
A comparative measure of a material's gritty uncomfortableness and ability to get everywhere (especially where unwanted) despite the most stringent of precautions

SANGOBEG *interj.* :
The final line of a traditional Japanese morality tale. It is uttered with triumphant disdain by a long-oppressed servant when his master (in some versions a European) receives his come-uppance and is driven, penniless, from his home and estates

SANNOX *n.* :
Long-discontinued 1920's lavatory cleaning product

SATLY *adv.* :
In the sitting position (e.g. '...Edna rested, satly, in the drawing room... ')

SAWBRIDGE *n.* :
A technique used by sappers to slow an advancing enemy before the development of safe, powerful explosives

SCAFELL PIKE *n.* :
Tool used to secure the footings of temporary access

structures which have to be erected on muddy ground in order to facilitate the construction and maintenance of buildings. The device comprises a metre-long tapered spike with four 500cm blades mounted longitudinally at right-angles to each other at its wider end (like the flights on a dart), which prevent lateral movement. The spikes are driven into the ground leaving 500cm-long round shafts exposed. The lowest tubes of the support structure are mounted on these shafts

SCARCEWATER *n.* :
An oasis

SCHOLES *n.* :
Light flip-flop sandals made by a famous foot-care company

SCONSER *n.* :
A maker of decorative candle-holders

SCOT'S GAP *n.* :
The distance between the hem of a kilt and the top of the adjoining woolly socks (where the knees are usually kept)

SCOURIE *n.* :
Local Highland slang term for a green nylon pan-scrub

SEA PALLING *n.* :
A feeling commonly experienced after a week's

holiday on the coast during which it has done nothing but rain

SEAFORD *n.* :
Where the Israelites actually made their escape from the Egyptians (Egyptian artefacts are reputedly still washed up on the beach)

SEASCALE *n.* :
Imprecise term for salt deposited on coastal structures by flying spray

SEEND *v.* :
(arch.) Old Wiltshire word, the past tense of the verb 'see'

SELLY OAK *n.* :
Ancient tree under which one of the earliest recorded annual produce markets first took place

SELWORTHY *adj.* :
Suitable to put on eBay

SEMER *n.* :
The lowest of the skilled grades of worker in the UK cotton mills of the mid-19th century

SETON MAINS *v.* :
Specific technical term used in the planning approvals process, meaning to connect a remote property to the electricity, gas and water grids

SEVEN WELLS *n.* :
A place where visitors are well advised to watch their step

SEWORGAN *n.* :
(1) Name given by its inventor, in its patent, to the first treadle-operated sewing machine; (2) Party game played, blindfold, by consultant surgeons

SHACKERSTONE *n.* :
Had there been a fourth Little Pig, this is undoubtedly the house it would have built for itself

SHADER *n.* :
From the earliest Daguerreotype in 1839, artists were quick to add colour to monochrome photographs by hand-painting them. This soon led to an industry of professional 'shaders' colouring the images captured by amateur photographers. The service was finally made redundant with the introduction of 'Kodachrome' film in the mid-20th century

SHAFTENHOE END *n.* :
The metal blade (originally of wrought-iron, later steel) for a long-handled weeding tool

SHAP *n.* :
(arch.) Ancient Cumbrian term meaning the singular of sheep

SHARPENHOE *v.*:
The process of putting a fine-edge onto a shaftenhoe end (qv.). Wrought-iron blades were usually sharpened with a file and relatively quickly lost their edge. Steel blades were most often sharpened using a grindstone and, if tempered and case-hardened by a skilled blacksmith, would stay sharp for much longer

SHAUGH PRIOR *interj.*:
A way of agreeing with the Abbot of one's monastery which borders on the disrespectful

SHEEPY MAGNA *n.*:
Traditional signage at North of England sheep sales indicating the pens for ewes and tups

SHEEPY PARVA *n.*:
Traditional signage at North of England sheep sales indicating the pens for lambs

SHEERNESS *n.*:
System of measurement for fine cloth, combining the measures of weight (per area), smoothness and thread diameter in a single metric. The higher the sheerness-number, the finer the cloth

SHEINTON *interj.*:
A phrase often heard when contacting retail outlets in London (by phone or in person) and asking for a female assistant/customer service advisor/agent/ etc., with whom one has been dealing before

SHELLOW BOWELLS *n.* :
Lay (non-medical) term for rectal prolapse

SHILLINGFORD St GEORGE *interj.* :
Cry of today's UKIP on-street fund-raisers equating to the apolitical chant "A Penny for the Guy" of previous centuries

SHIPBOURNE *v.* :
Carried by sea

SHOTTLE *n.* :
A proprietary sized bottle, particular to a well-known schoft drinks company

SHURLOCK ROW *n.* :
Mrs. Hudson's private opinion of the Great Detective's violin playing

SHUT HEATH *n.* :
Originally an area of common land renamed after the General Inclosure Act of 1845

SILPHO *n.* :
A popular 19th century dieting aid

SIMPRIM *n.* :
Android app which deletes all user data from a SIM-card without having to perform a full Factory Reset, thereby removing all the settings as well

SINFIN *n.* :
Name given to the putative great white man-

eating cod of the North Sea. Said to be a mutation caused by the outflow from the Sellafield nuclear reprocessing plant, sightings have been reported from as far afield as the Faroes, the Shetland Islands, coastal Norway and Great Yarmouth. It is said by fisher-folk that during the autumn, winter and spring, the creature scours the fishing grounds of the North Sea waiting to overpower careless trawlers that foul their nets, whilst in the summer it cruises the inshore waters off the British east-coast holiday resorts waiting to snap up any incautious bather. Concerningly, experts agree that taking into account the timing of the various sightings, if any two are confirmed, then there must be more than one of these monsters out there

SINNARHARD *n.* :
A granite hassock prescribed by priests as part of the penance process for those whose misdeeds were particularly dire or who demonstrated tiresomely recidivistic tendencies in their wrongdoings. Malefactors would be expected to spend several hours kneeling on their sinnarhard each Sunday praying for forgiveness or contemplating the error of their ways

SIXPENNY HANDLEY *n.* :
Erotic diversion offered to soldiers on leave during WW1 in the less genteel parts of our great cities

SLACK HEAD *n.* :
Condition sometimes suffered by those too fond of alcohol

SKINIDIN *n.* :
The excited squeaks, giggles and roars produced by a mixed group of inexperienced skinny-dippers – especially in climates not well suited to the activity

SLIDDERY *adj.* :
Possessed of a very low coefficient of friction

SMALL DOLE *n.* :
The Unemployment Benefit paid to a person with even the most meagre savings

SMOO *interj.* :
A sound made (usually rather huskily) by a cow that is after something

SOCKBURN *n.* :
Stiff, glazed finish found on cotton and polyamide hose left in a tumble dryer for too long

SOMPTING *n.* :
An object, never effectively described, found in the way she moves

SOUND MUIR *n.* :
(arch.) 19th century Scottish term for a speaking trumpet

SOUTH ZEAL *n.* :
A faint herd instinct, recently detected in human populations in the Northern Hemisphere, to move to, or have holiday homes, nearer the Equator

SPARROWPIT *n.* :
A shallow dusty depression in the ground where small birds, of many types, preen and clean their feathers – unless there has been recent rain

SPARROWS GREEN *n.* :
Erroneous entry in a novice twitcher's log-book – in all probability they were greenfinches

SPELLBROOK *n.* :
Examination question intended to encourage students who, shall we say, particularly need encouragement

SPENNYMOOR *interj.* :
Cry of a market trader when a customer, who has become aware that they are being sold 'market weighton' (qv.), seeks to get their revenge by means of short payment

SPEXHALL *n.* :
(1) A very large optician's shop – that is, the very large shop of an optician, not the shop of a very large optician; (2) The name of the country-house head office of an international engineering standards organisation

SPLATT *v.* :
What happens when an object is placed under strain for which it is structurally inadequate

SPLOTTLANDS *v.* :
A particular instance of splatt (qv.); when a structurally weak object (e.g. a bird dropping) comes into contact with: a human being, a window, the ground, etc.

SPOFFORTH *interj.* :
An impolite Yorkshire expression suggesting that someone should go away – equivalent to the more widespread bu***r-off

SPRINGWELL *n.* :
The original name proposed for Zebedee in the *Magic Roundabout*

SPROUGHTON *v.* :
The least popular step in serving a Christmas dinner (well, except for Beverley – don't ask!)

SPYWAY *n.* :
The trade association of private detectives

St JUST *n.* :
Ancient village recorded in the Domesday Book as St Justin's. Recent archaeological evidence suggests that sometime during the Middle Ages the arm of a fingerpost on the nearby drovers' trail pointing to the village rotted and the end

dropped off. At that time only clerics and the very wealthy could read so the error remained unnoticed for several generations. Despite efforts by the Parish it was by then far too late to rectify the situation

STAINDROP *n.* :
The basic quantum of dirty rain or a splashed puddle

STAINLAND *n.* :
The trade name of a specialist varnish business

STANFREE *n.* :
The release from prison of Stanley Crook (qv.); his freedom being a source of periodic merriment in his community

STANLEY CROOK *n.* :
An incorrigible, though frequently apprehended, criminal

STANSBATCH *n.* :
The group of rascals released at the same time as Stanley Crook (qv.) on any given occasion. It was customary to invite them to the stanfree (qv.) celebrations

STAPLE CROSS *n.* :
Two paper-fasteners inserted at right-angles for greater strength

STARCROSS *n.* :
Shakespeare's original setting for *Romeo & Juliet*

STARLINGS GREEN *n.* :
Another mistaken entry by that unhappy twitcher – on this occasion almost certainly parrots

STARTFORTH *v.* :
(1) To set out; (2) To react very sluggishly to a starting pistol

STAWELL *interj.* :
Friendly valediction between acquaintances once common in Somerset

STAXIGOE *interj.* :
A piece of slurred, barely intelligible, information passed on from someone near the front door towards the end of a party, meaning "He's missed his cab."

STEELE ROAD *n.* :
The terms in which the first reports of the Stockton to Darlington railway were delivered in the Borders region

STEEPLE BUMPSTEAD *n.* :
The Steeple Bumpstead as he became known, was a kindly, good-natured Essex villager with learning difficulties born in 1789. In his mid-teens he fell deeply in love with Letitia, a local girl whose mother did the flower arrangements at the

parish church. Gently rejected by Letitia as being a simpleton, he would nevertheless regularly hide in the belfry, adoringly watching Letitia and her mother setting up the flowers for the Sunday services. One Sunday, arriving early, as he did, to take up his position to pump the organ, he noticed to his horror that, whilst the flowers in the body of the church were beautiful, all the floral decorations beyond the altar step were dead; the flowers just dried stalks and twigs. Seeking to warn his beloved and her mother and spare them any embarrassment he rushed to the top of the tower and, as he saw them coming, cried out as loudly as he could, "The Sanctuary. The Sanctuary." In so doing, he overbalanced and fell to the path below. Cradled in Letitia's arms he gasped an explanation of his actions. "Yes, my dearest," Letitia replied, "it's called Ikebana." "Ah," he wheezed, and with a wistful smile, expired. Some say that this event was the inspiration for Victor Hugo's later story, *The Hunchback of Notre Dame*. There is no evidence for this and it is difficult to see why anyone would choose to recount such a dismal tale

STEPASIDE *n.* :
Novelty dance briefly popular during the 'Roaring Twenties' along with the Charleston, Black-bottom and others. As with most such dances of the period, dancers probably needed to be 'roaring' to do it

STOCK GREEN *n.* :
Bacon which is past its sell-by date

STODY *adj.* :
Something which is like a very large and ugly frog

STOKE ASH *v.* :
Suffolk dialect expression for doing something which is pointless. The analogy uses the idea that to stoke a fire/boiler with its own burnt ash is a waste of time and effort (cf. carrying coals to Newcastle)

STOVEN *adj.* :
(1) Of something placed in an oven; (2) Of something crushed

STRAITON *n.* :
Seeking to 'jump on the bandwagon' of success created by the Stepaside (qv.) this contemporaneous dance was devised by a competing band-leader. Somewhat similar in concept to the more recent 'March of the Mods', like many contrived entertainments it foundered with barely a ripple

STRATFORD TONY *n.* :
East-end gangster famous during the 1950s. Much of the information about Tony is probably apocryphal as he is popularly seen as a latter-day Robin Hood, the villain with a heart of gold that one might find in an Ealing comedy. Whichever was his true character it clearly demonstrated the value of good PR

STREET DINAS *n.*
Pavement cafés

STUCKTON *adj.* :
Attached with adhesive

STYAL *n.* :
Commoners may have style, but Royals have styal (or in some cases don't)

STYRRUP *n.* :
Soothing unguent used to alleviate the soreness and bruising of the instep experienced by determined jockeys and novice riders. Often used by 'horsey' people to refer to any sort of salve or balm

SUNBURY *n.* :
(arch.) Old Surrey term for sunset

SURREX *n.* :
Embryonic county which never developed

SUTTON ON SEA *n.* :
An only partially successful attempt at land reclamation

SWAN GREEN *n.* :
Oh dear! This poor twitcher clearly has some sort of eye problem or forgotten to take his/her sunglasses off

SWANAGE *n.* :
This term may reasonably be classed as 'royal

slang'. In 1482, Edward IV, by Royal Charter, granted the Vintners' and Dyers' Companies the right to own and mark swans on those stretches of the Thames reserved for the Crown (albeit under the watchful eye of the monarch's Swan Marker). Shortly after, Henry VIII, never one to allow money, food or drink to slip between his fingers, is said to have lamented his predecessor's action saying, that "…he has squandered our God-given right of swanage to a parcel of men of little account or worth… ". Amongst conflicting theories, this is considered to be the most likely explanation for the genesis of the word, as no one but a monarch would have dared to refer to a Royal Charter by anything other than its full title. Further credence may be inferred from court records that show in that year, the King's jester, Will 'Sunshine' Merrymarch, penned an entertainment comprising a 'saucie song', and that during the singing of its chorus, Will would run around the room whilst selected courtiers would try to strike him with inflated pigs' bladders on sticks. Only a snatch of the chorus has survived which runs, '…swanage, how I love you, how I love you, my dear old swanage… '

SWANLEY *adj.* :
Term sometimes applied to leaders and public figures of many sorts when 'in a corner'; it suggests behaviour calm and unruffled on the surface while paddling furiously out of sight

SWAY *n.* :
A dance which was yet another contemporary attempt to cash in on the Stepaside (qv.) – no more successful than the Straiton (qv.)

SWORDLY *adv.* :
In the manner of a sword. Thus stage directions for actors in films like *Star Wars* might read '… stooping, he grasps a light-sabre and waves it about swordly…'

SYDLING St NICHOLAS *n.* :
A petty criminal, well known to both police and public alike, who frequents fairs and High Streets in Dorset in the run-up to Christmas. Disguising himself as Santa, he will edge up to his victim before snatching the 'valuable' that is his target and run off; he is not above snatching a child's toy, recently received from one of the legitimate 'Sitting St Nicholases' to be found in many large stores. In practice, this villain's advancing years and cumbersome disguise cause him to be regularly 'brought to book' by passers-by or even his child victims, without any assistance from the police. Because of his manifest ineptitude, 'Sydling St Nick' is beginning to become an established part of the Christmas scene in his area and may yet become a celebrity

T

TADWORTH *adj.* :
Of little value

TAIBACH *n.* :
Welsh term for a ribbon, piece of material or similar used to secure an open curtain tidily and decoratively

TALLENTIRE *adj.* :
Used of something that can be dismantled, meaning it is particularly high when considered altogether (e.g. A courtier viewing Charles I's beheaded corpse might well have observed "…yes, although he was tallentire…")

TANGLEY *adj.* :
Liable, very easily, to become inextricably confused and knotted

TANSOR *n.* :
Probably the least pleasant effect of too much exposure to the sun

TARPORLEY *adj.* :
During the 19th and early 20th century a popular remedy for someone with 'a chesty cough' was

to sleep in a room with a lighted 'Wright's Coal-tar Evaporator' (this was a metal can containing a tea-light underneath a ceramic dish containing coal-tar). Anyone considered ill enough for such treatment was considered 'tarporley'

TAVERNSPITE *n.* :
The unreasonable and unreasoning violent anger that can occur in people who have consumed far too much alcohol (most commonly demonstrated on Friday and Saturday nights)

TAXAL *adj.* :
Relating to, or having to do with, tax. Not, as the urban legend would have it, the motto carved over the front door lintel inside No.11 Downing Street

TAYINLOAN *n.* :
Scottish term for a particular kind of domestic debt. Originally it referred to a small quantity of a household's tea lent out to a neighbour, but soon extended to cover any sort of domestic substance (e.g. a cup of sugar). It was common for a note to be made of this which was surrendered to the debtor when the loan was repaid

TENDRING *n.* :
Offered by the GPO (as it then was) in the 1920s and '30s, the Tendring Service was initially intended to be an aid for hard of hearing telephone users, but it was quickly adopted by money-rich time-poor subscribers. When the operator connected a call to

a Tendring subscriber she (and it always was she) would count the number of times the phone rang. After the tenth ring, she would interrupt the call and invite the caller to leave a message which she then would make repeated attempts to deliver

TESTWOOD *n.* :

In bowls (lawn bowls), the captain of each team carries with them a testwood. This is a completely 'true' unweighted wood which, before the match, either team (most usually the visitors) may use, once per team member, to evaluate the 'run' of the green. The national association holds the National Testwood; made of *lignum vitae* with an adjustable lead core, it is considerably heavier than a match-bowl and its balance is checked, every leap-year, at the National Physical Laboratory. In the event of an inter-club dispute, the association's inspectors will visit a green and, using the National Testwood, evaluate its 'truth' (levelness). In the event of a further appeal, a ramp may be used to deliver the Testwood

THE NEUK *n.* :

Target for a daring and imaginative intelligence operation during the Cold War. MI5 conceived a plan where diplomats and politicians, when at events attended by Russians would, just occasionally, refer to this location pronouncing it 'the nuke'. It was expected that this would entice hostile operatives to the area, making them easier to identify and reducing their effectiveness elsewhere. Whether this had any effect (even on the local B&B industry or property prices) is unknown

THOMASTOWN *n.* :
Name proposed for a community to form part of the television adaptation of the Rev. W Awdrey's *Thomas the Tank Engine* books. It was dropped as being too unfaithful to the original (which is quite an appropriate judgement relating to a work by a cleric)

THONG *n.* :
Narrow strip of material (usually leather) used for binding, tying, whipping etc., – though recently given the more specific meaning of a Netherthong (qv.)

THORNAGE *adj.* :
The non-calibrated measure of the 'spikiness' of a shrub (e.g. '…despite his protestations, Brer Rabbit was not in the least surprised by the thornage of the bush in which he found himself…')

THORNICOMBE *n.* :
Grooming implement more closely resembling a hair-brush than a comb, having short, sharp, inflexible, widely separated bristles set in a flat, rectangular wooden hand-grip. Used to comb out tangles in long hair or wool

THORNS *n.* :
The one village that should have a pub called The Crown, which apparently doesn't

THREE CROSSES *n.* :
One of the most classical arrangements for crosses

THRUMSTER *n.* :
Common 'trade-term' for the rhythm guitar player in a pop group

TINTAGEL *n.* :
(WWII RAF slang) A prosthetic male member

TIXALL *adj.* :
(of something that) Meets all the requirements

TIXOVER *v.* :
(of an internal combustion engine) Idles

TONYPANDY *n.* :
Andy's brother. Though never referred to in the series, always Looby Loo's favourite. The two brothers still don't speak

TOPROW *n.* :
The very cheapest seats in a traditionally designed theatre

TORROBULL *n.* :
Fighting bull, imported from Spain as a novel attraction at Highland games

TOWCESTER *n.* :
Whoever is currently making a speech at a wedding reception

TOWEDNACK *n.* :
The skill of hauling a caravan or trailer

TRADESPARK *n.* :
National wholesale electrical supplier

TRE-GROES *n.* :
Remarkably large horticultural grow-bags

TREDEGAR *v.* :
To 'step out' with enthusiasm

TRELIGHTS *n.* :
Christmas decorations

TREVALYN *n.* :
Vera's husband?

TRIMDON *n.* :
An unusually well-groomed college fellow

TROSSACHS *n.* :
That part of a man's anatomy most sensitive to cold breezes when he is wearing a kilt or shorts

TROWAY *adj.* :
Disposable

TRUNCH *n.* :
Abbreviated term for truncheon (similar, for example, to lunch – luncheon)

TRURO *n.* :
The straight course steered by a skilled oarsman (rather than the meandering dog-legs of an amateur)

TUFFLEY *adv.* :
Subject to difficult and demanding circumstances (e.g. '…she believed that all children should be brought up tuffley…')

TURNERS PUDDLE *n.* :
One of J.M.W.Turner's earlier and least well known works; it has not been seen in public since 1785 (possibly because the buyer's heirs feel he paid 'over the odds' for a primitive, pre-seminal, work)

TUSHINGHAM-CUM-GRINDLEY *n.* :
(Author's note:- I feel that speculation about this place is likely to take the publication to a place where it should not go) (Agreed. Ed.)

TY-NANT *n.* :
Extremely rare insect found only in the North East of England

TYNDRUM *n.* :
Child's toy which, if popular with its owner, is at

least as loud, annoying and disagreeable as the real thing. What is worse, being tin, unlike the real thing it cannot be broken over the head of the player

U

UCKFIELD *n.*:
A farmer's plot that has recently been visited by the muck-spreader

UFTON *v.*:
What happened to the houses of the Three Little Pigs

UGLEY *adj.*:
The characteristic of language ascribed by Hollywood to early hominids

UISKEN *v.*:
Beaten (as an egg, for example)

ULCEBY SKITTER *n.*:
The first tell-tale outward symptom of a lesion in the gut

ULLOCK *n.*:
The animal from which eef is produced

UNDER RIVER *n.*:
(1) (arch.) drowned; (2) (more recently) flooded

UNSTONE *n.* :
Largely ineffective reprieve order from a fundamentalist mis-trial

UNDERBARROW *n.* :
Almost always a wheel

UP EXE *interj.* :
View sometimes expressed by recent divorcees

UP SYDLING *v.* :
Surreptitious approach technique used, with varying levels of success, by Sydling St Nicholas (qv.)

UPHILL *n.* :
Settlement named by its residents (who must surely have been unreasonably pessimistic) in apparent denial of the fact that it must be downhill on the way back, (qv. Downhill; is there a regional characteristic displayed here?)

UPLODERS *n.* :
Those few who chose to contribute to the Internet rather than simply trying to fill their empty lives by sucking it dry

UPLOWMAN *interj.* :
(1) (arch.) A hail from a landed personage seeking to attract the attention of one of their agricultural workers; (2) (arch.) Command from a 'person of rank' wishing to spare a commoner the discomfort of kneeling

UPPER HILL *n.* :
The place where, traditionally, Jack and Jill went

UPPER LYE *n.* :
Old military term for the top bunk

UPWELL *prep.* :
Water which has been drawn (e.g. '…they slaked their thirst with the upwell water before lowering the bucket once again…')

URRAY *interj.* :
Phonetically accurate spelling for most cheers

V

VATSETTER *n.* :
A little-known official title of the Chancellor of the Exchequer

W

WAKEFIELD *n.* :
Area of electro-magnetic disturbance caused by the passage of a high-energy charged particle

WALBUTT *n.* :
cf. *The Complete Kama Sutra*, Section 2, Chapter 5

WALDITCH *n.* :
First found around Bronze-age dwellings, a trench to drain away ground-water and prevent it from entering the hut. Over time this developed into a defensive feature culminating in castle moats and the English Channel

WANTAGE *n.* :
A collective term used by psychologists to encompass all the elements in Abraham Maslow's Hierarchy of Needs (Physiology, Security, Social, Self-esteem, Self-actualisation). (e.g. '…thus a deficiency in any one of these elements may be perceived by the subject as a deficit of the total wantage balance, leading, mistakenly, to action intended to increase the levels of a wantage-element entirely unconnected to the source of the disturbance…')

WARCOP *n.*:
Now a largely forgotten comic-book hero. A military policeman who volunteered for nuclear experiments which left him with super-powers. Though immensely strong, armoured and with X-ray vision, he never really gained popularity as all he did was break up fights between drunken servicemen in bars

WARLABY *n.*:
The wallaby, as first reported to American newspaper readers

WARMSWORTH *n.*:
An unexpectedly reasonable energy bill

WARNINGLID *n.*:
'Pop-up' metal lid as found on jam-jars and the like

WARTHERMASKE *n.*:
The facial disguise, not unlike today's 'Anonymous' masks, that weather-man Michael Fish was obliged to wear in public for several months, to avoid abuse, after his "There is no hurricane on the way" prediction in 1987. The Met. Office retains the original mask for the next forecaster who needs it

WARTLING *n.*:
A small skin blemish

WATCHET *Interj.*:
A warning shout

WATERFOOT *n.* :
A frequent complication of 'water on the knee'

WATERHEAD *n.* :
One of several 'lay' names for the ailment, hydrocephalus – fluid on the brain, most commonly referred to as 'water on the brain'. Popularly believed to be cured by a tap on the head. (Author's note: my thanks to whichever Music Hall artist cracked that first)

WAVERBRIDGE *n.* :
Short-lived London nickname for the Millennium Footbridge across the Thames until such time as it was rectified

WEEDON *n.* :
Gardening chemical to promote the growth of wild flowers

WELBURY *interj.* :
The traditional cry of the last player of a game of Bury St Edmunds (qv.) left standing. He or she is necessarily the winner

WELDON BRIDGE *n.* :
Prefabricated support structure constructed by Isambard Kingdom Brunel and applied to the iron bridge at Ironbridge to protect it from squeezing forces caused by the gradual inward movement of the sides of the gorge. Though removed some years later following remedial earthworks, inward

pressure on the bridge remains a problem to this day

WELLAND *interj.* :
Worcestershire argot roughly meaning 'so what'

WELTON *v.* :
To carry out a very thorough shoe repair

WENDOVER *n.* :
The place you arrive at the end of a long and aimless walk

WEST DUNNET *interj.* :
A 'catchphrase' from Compton Flaxstead's series of 'novels for boys', published during the 1920s, recounting the lives of pupils at the fictional academy of Wellworth Cramming. The character, West, the school's principal picton (qv.), was, predictably, constantly in trouble, visited upon him by various groups of co-pupils (ranging from 'his chums' to the entire school) chanting this catchphrase as soon as they were asked, by the Head, Dr. Knottjolly. Little toe-rags

WEST YOKE *n.* :
Term used by 17th cent. carters for the left-hand place in a harness for two oxen (from the point of view of the animals). It should be noted that there was never an East Yoke which was always referred to as 'Tother. By the end of the century, along the South Coast (especially near naval ports) the term

had fallen into disuse being replaced by Port Yoke, though 'Tother was retained

WHERWELL *n.* :
A supernatural entity said to haunt a small Hampshire community. With the coming of mains water the old village well in the market square was almost completely back-filled (for safety) and converted into an ornamental fountain. Yet occasionally, on moonless nights, it is said that its natural roots call to it and it escapes its modern confines and, seeking vengeance for its incarceration, roams the square in search of human victims. This 'curse' is most strongly attested to by the village aldwincle (qv.) whenever he is found in the fountain after the pubs have shut

WHINNIE LIGGATE *n.* :
A community which, despite its many other claims to fame, is best known for being the inspiration for a limerick, which goes as follows:-

> *There once was a girl, Winnie Liggate*
> *Who found herself trapped on a frigate*
> *She appealed to the Jacks*
> *Who loosened their slacks*
> *At which point the tale turns explicit*

WHITBARROW *n.* :
Small hand-cart or trolley used to carry relics and altar-ware during early-summer religious processions

WHITE LADIES ASTON *n.* :
A very ill-advised item headline in Auto Trader

WHITEROW *n.* :
Extremely loud white-noise

WIDE OPEN *n.* :
A North East community 'in sore need of a good marshal'

WILBY *n.* :
There are two adjacent villages called Wilby, one in Norfolk, one in Suffolk. This probably proves that 'whatever wilby, wilby'

WINCOBANK *n.* :
A financial institution targeting its services on senior Air Force officers

WINFARTHING *n.* :
The pay-out on an incredibly short-odds bet

WINLESS *n.* :
The stake-money on an incredibly short-odds bet which loses

WIRRAL *n.* :
The town which inspired Sir Cliff Richard to write the hit theme-song to the film *Summer Holiday*

WOOD EATON *n.* :
Site of a substantial copse once standing adjacent

to the place where beavers have recently been re-introduced to the UK

WOODBRIDGE *n.* :
A river crossing susceptible to demolition using the sawbridge technique (qv.)

YARDLEY HASTINGS *v phr.* :
To repeatedly run very fast but only for a very short distances (commonly demonstrated by people who have made 'take more exercise' their New Year's resolution)

YARMOUTH *n.* :
A particularly voluble Sloane-ranger

YIELDEN *v.* :
(arch.) Given-up, lost (e.g. '…all ye landes south of said brooke were yielden…')

YOKER *n.* :
Job title of a role to be found in the first process of a meringue factory

Z

ZEAL MONACHORUM *n.* :
(1) The place of foundation of the eponymous order of monks and the site of its sole monastery. The order was founded by Zealous Ambleforth, who was initially a postulant, then novice at a nearby Gilbertine monastery. During his novitiate, the Novice Director realised that, due to the fact that he was tone deaf (unable to sing even the simplest plain-chant) and colour blind, Zealous could never rise above the Novitiate. Sensing his sincerity and depth of faith, the Director advised Zealous to go out into the world and find where the Spirit called him. Less than five miles down the road, Zealous was bidden to establish an order of the most simple and pious nature, dedicated principally to doing good in the community whilst celebrating its profound faith without the trappings of tune or colour. Thus was founded the community of Zeal Monachorum. The order was often referred to as the 'Red Monks' due to the colour of their habit. Perceived by the Brothers as a mute and restful green in harmony with the rest of Creation, to most of humanity it appeared an eye-wateringly vivid scarlet. The order flourished briefly but its ultimate demise was due, simply, to

a shortage of tone-deaf, colour-blind men wishing to become monks. (2) The name was subsequently adopted by a small clique of Royalists during the English Civil War

Acknowledgements

I would like to express my thanks to several people for their part in the creation of this book.

I am grateful to my four children; Michael, Andrew, Rachael and Gregory, not only for their consistent enthusiasm and encouragement but also for periodically reading and critiquing the text as it has developed. Gregory deserves thanks too for helping me to 'plough' through lists of place names looking for locations that might be suitable inclusion. He also provided the verse.

I should also thank my sister, Kate and my cousin, Jane. Though busy with books of their own they made time to encourage me and to provide me with specialist inputs. Kate's artistic abilities helped no-end with the cover design, whilst Jane provided welcome historical guidance.

In order to protect the innocent I must then add that if there are any historical inaccuracies in the book (and I know of at least one) they are entirely mine, either by accident or design.